BLOOD HONEY

BLOOD HONEY

CHANA BLOCH

Autumn House Press

PITTSBURGH

Autumn House Press Staff
Executive Editor and Founder: Michael Simms
Executive Director: Richard St. John
Community Outreach Director: Michael Wurster
Co-Director: Eva-Maria Simms
Fiction Editor: Sharon Dilworth
Coal Hill Editor: Joshua Storey
Associate Editors: Anna Catone, Laurie Mansell Reich,
   Rebecca Clever, Philip Terman
Fulfillment Manager: Bernadette James
Assistant Editors: Carolyne Whelan, Evan Oare
Editorial Consultant: Ziggy Edwards
Media Consultant: Jan Beatty
Tech Crew Chief: Michael Milberger

This project was supported by the Pennsylvania Council on the Arts, a state agency, through its regional arts funding partnership, Pennsylvania Partners in the Arts (PPA). State government funding comes through an annual appropriation by Pennsylvania's General Assembly. PPA is administered in Allegheny County by Greater Pittsburgh Arts Council.

ISBN: 978-1-932870-33-6
Library of Congress: 2009930674

for Dave

You speak to me. I trust your voice
because it has lumps of hard pain in it
the way real honey
has lumps of wax from the honeycomb.

Yehuda Amichai

ALSO BY CHANA BLOCH

Poetry
Mrs. Dumpty
The Past Keeps Changing
The Secrets of the Tribe

Translation
Yehuda Amichai, *Open Closed Open* (with Chana Kronfeld)
Yehuda Amichai, *The Selected Poetry* (with Stephen Mitchell)
Dahlia Ravikovitch, *Hovering at a Low Altitude: The Collected Poetry* (with Chana Kronfeld)
Dahlia Ravikovitch, *The Window: New and Selected Poems* (with Ariel Bloch)
Dahlia Ravikovitch, *A Dress of Fire*
The Song of Songs (with Ariel Bloch)

Scholarship
Spelling the Word: George Herbert and the Bible

ACKNOWLEDGMENTS

Grateful thanks to the editors of the following publications in which these poems have appeared, many in earlier versions or with different titles:

Alaska Quarterly: "The Daily News," "The Sixth Trumpet"
Coal Hill Review: "Anteroom"
FIELD: "Flour and Ash," "A Mantle"
Forward: "Tashlich"
Kenyon Review: "Brothers," "The Sixth Age"
Lyric Poetry Review: "Tell Me"
Michigan Quarterly Review: "The New World," "The Dark of Day"
New Orleans Review: "The Weight"
Prairie Schooner (winner of a 2006 Glenna Luschei Prairie Schooner
    Award): "Covenant," "Sweeping Up," "Mirror, Mirror," "Trespass,"
    "Private Lives," "Envy," "A Show of Red"
Poetry: "The Messiah of Harvard Square"
Runes: "Sixty O'Clock," "Curb"
Salmagundi: "Woman Talk"
Southern Poetry Review: "Reprieve," "The Grand Canyon,"
    "Salvage," "Green, Green," "A Buried Language," "The Known
    Facts," "Roots"
Threepenny Review: "The Discipline of Marriage"
TriQuarterly: "The Dead of Night," "A Long Winter's Night,"
    "A Life on Earth"
Tikkun: "The Spoils," "Power," "Blood Honey"

Blood Honey won the 2004 Alice Fay Di Castagnola Award of the Poetry Society of America for a manuscript-in-progress, selected by Jane Hirshfield.

"The New World" and "The Dark of Day" are reprinted in *Jewish in America*, ed. Sara Blair and Jonathan Freedman (University of Michigan Press, 2004), and in *When She Named Fire: An Anthology of Contemporary Poetry by American Women*, ed. Andrea Hollander Budy (Autumn House Press, 2009).

"Natural History" appears in *The Addison Street Anthology*, ed. Robert Hass and Jessica Fisher (Heyday Books, 2004).

"The Messiah of Harvard Square" is reprinted in the 2005 *Pushcart Prize XXIX: Best of the Small Presses.*

"The Discipline of Marriage" and "Portrait of the Artist" are included in *The Face of Poetry: Contemporary Portraits and Poems*, ed. Zack Rogow (University of California Press, 2005).

"The Sixth Age" is reprinted in *On Retirement*, ed. Robin Chapman and Judith Strasser (University of Iowa Press, 2007).

CONTENTS

I

THE NEW WORLD

My uncle killed a man and was proud of it.
Some punk with a knife came at him in Flatbush
and he knocked the sucker to the ground.
The sidewalk finished the job.

By then he'd survived two wives
and a triple bypass. He carried
a bit of the plastic tubing in his pocket
and would show it to anyone.
He'd unbutton his shirt right there on the street
and show off the scar.

As a boy, he watched a drunken Cossack
go after his father with an ax.
His sister tried to staunch the bleeding
with a hunk of dry bread.

That's the old country for you:
they ate with their hands, went hungry to bed,
slept in their stink. When pain knocked,
they opened the door.

The bitter drive to Brooklyn every Sunday
when I was a child—
Uncle George in the doorway snorting and laughing,
I'm gonna take a bite of your little behind.

He was a good-looker in a pin-striped suit
and shoeshine shoes.
This is America, we don't live
in the Dark Ages anymore, sweetie.
This is a free country.

TELL ME

Tell me the story where you hit your father.
I've heard it, but tell me again
how he'd come after you when he'd had too many,
how one day finally
you gave him what he asked for
and there he was—flat
on the kitchen floor.

You put the door behind you and started walking.
Your legs kept you moving from one block to the next
while the drone in your blood
mulled it over.

When you got back at midnight, your father
kept his mouth shut. You too.
The words that slept in that house
were homeless and hungry.
You had all learned to step around them.

Tell me that story. I wait for the part where
your whole hand
pronounces a single word
so unmistakable
there's no way to take it back.

It's a story from hell
but I like it. Lie down with me, love,
and tell it from the beginning.

POTATO EATERS

My grandmother never did learn to write.
"Making love" was not in her lexicon;
I wonder if she ever took off her clothes
when her husband performed his conjugal duties.
She said God was watching,
reciting Psalms was dependable medicine,
a woman in pants an abomination.

In their hut on the Dniester
six children scraped the daily potatoes from a single plate;
each one held a bare spoon.

Five years from the *shtetl* her daughters
disguise themselves
in lisle stockings and flapper dresses.
The boys slick their hair with pomade.
What do they remember of Russia? "Mud."

That's grandma in the center. At ease in owl glasses.
"Don't run, you'll fall."
Mostly she keeps her mouth shut; the children
would rather not hear.
What does a full stomach know
of an empty stomach?

It's time you opened your mouth, *bobbe*,
I'm old enough now to ask you a thing or two
and you're too dead to be annoyed.
You'll know where to find me,
I'm the daughter of your second son.
I have the spoons.

BROTHERS

When I was the Baba Yaga of the house
on my terrible chicken legs,
the children sat close on the sofa as I read,
both of them together
determined to be scared.

Careful! I cackled, stalking them
among the pillows:
You bad Russian boy,
I eat you up!
They shivered and squirmed, my delicious sons,

waiting for a mighty arm
to seize them.
I chased them screeching down the hall,
I catch you, I eat you!
my witch-blade hungry for the spurt
of laughter—

What stopped me
even as I lifted my hand?
The stricken voice that cried: *Eat him!*
Eat my brother.

THE MESSIAH OF HARVARD SQUARE

Every year some student would claim to be the Messiah.
It was the rabbi who had to deal with them.
He had jumped, years ago, from a moving boxcar
on the way to a death camp. That leap
left him ready for anything.

This year at Pesach, a Jewish student proclaimed
Armageddon. "Burn the books! Burn the textbooks!"
he shouted to a cheerful crowd,
sang Hebrew songs to confuse the Gentiles,
dressed for the end like Belshazzar.
People stopped to whisper and laugh.

"I have a noble task," the boy explained.
"I must prepare myself to endure
the laughter of fools."

The rabbi was a skeptic.
Years ago he'd been taught, If you're planting a tree
and someone cries out, *The Messiah has come!*
finish planting the tree. Then
go see if it's true.

Still, he took the boy into his study
and questioned him slowly, meticulously,
as if the poor soul before him might be,
God help us, the Messiah.

REPRIEVE

We were drinking coffee in her pre-war flat,
four walls, Pompeiian gray
to match her complexion.
An old Jewish woman in Prague.
Her dead husband laughing in a dapper suit,
fedora, cigarette, one arm around a life
flash-frozen and set at the table
beside the Czech pastries.

She held me with her skinny hand.
"I could have left after the war with my baby
and started over." And then,
half to herself: "Did I make a mistake?"
Her baby was translating
into a broken German I could manage.

What a question to ask a green girl like me,
still too married to regret a marriage
I thought I chose.
Still three or four wars away from knowing
when a question
isn't a question, just a gasp of loss—
but mine to translate.

She poured coffee, passed the *kolacky*, awaited
my verdict. Yes, you should have left.
No, you did the right thing.

As if one could reprieve a life even now
by pointing a finger
left or right.

FLOUR AND ASH

"Make flour into dough," she answers,
"and fire will turn it into food.
Ash is the final abstraction of matter.
You can just brush it away."

She tacks a sheet of paper to the wall,
dips her hand in a palette of flour and ash,
applies the fine soft powders with a fingertip,
highlighting in chalk and graphite,
blending, blurring with her thumb.
Today she is working in seven shades of gray.

Outside the door, day lilies
in the high flush of summer-
about-to-be-fall. Her garden burns
red and yellow in the dry August air
and is not consumed.

Inside, on the studio wall, a heavy
particulate smoke
thickens and rises. Footsteps grime the snow.
The about-to-be-dead line up on the ramp
with their boxy suitcases,
ashen shoes.

When I get too close she yanks me back.
She hovers over her creation
though she too has a mind
to brush against that world
and wipe it out.

COVENANT

in memory of Paul Celan

What he was given was too hot to touch.
Live coal, glowing from the altar.

He took it
in the tongs of metaphor
so it wouldn't burn.

But it did burn. He reached for it
anyway. Slowly.
Slowly.

His poems were a miracle
of perversity. They knew before he did
what words give

and words take away.
How they slake
and inflame. How they salt
every morsel they save.

He left a place at the table
for the silence
that pressed a burning coal
to his lips.

POWER

"Why can't they just get along?" says my neighbor
when he hears the numbers on the morning news.
Then he's got the answer:
"They're people, that's why."

Thus saith my neighbor
who lets his Doberman out to bark at midnight
and grumbles "Yeah, yeah"
when I call to complain.

Meanwhile, in the precincts of power,
the new Chief of Staff
who learned his trade as a fighter pilot
is fending off questions from his swivel chair.

"And what did you feel," the reporters ask,
"when you dropped a bomb from an F-16?"
"I felt a slight lift of the wing," he says.
"After a second it passed."

THE SPOILS

The mother of Sisera looked out at a window,
and cried through the lattice.
Judges 5:28

An Israeli soldier, just back from the war,
gave me a photo he found of a mother and son,
a talisman the enemy wore to battle
in his khaki shirt pocket.
Forty years ago.

I was too giddy to ask
what he thought he was offering that day
—a trophy? a souvenir?
All he wanted, he said, was to get home safe.

His mother, my neighbor, fought the war
by candlelight in a Jerusalem shelter,
stood up, sat down,
clung to the phone like Sisera's mother:
Why is his chariot so long in coming?
Why tarry his nine hundred chariots of iron?
Surely the victors are dividing the spoils—

Home safe, the soldier let me take
a shot of him holding his dazed mother,
a shot of him cradling his gun.

Then he gave me the photo he found
in a dead man's pocket
and I took that too.

SONG WITHOUT WORDS

The Thai policeman laughed as he pointed
to the sole standing house. A tsunami laugh.
There is only one left, he said
and made that peculiar primate sound.
A high-pitched fending-off song
spiked with horror.

I laughed when they told me Hank broke his neck
diving from the jetty in Rockaway.
I had nothing to say.
That story was too hard for a thirteen-year-old,
it broke on a stone
in my throat.

There are hardly stops enough on the windpipe
for a human song. Laughing and coughing,
water sputtering out of my nostrils,
I covered my face.

This is the way it happens:
People are drowning, gulping, gasping,
reaching for a slippery plank
you let go of
your fistful of words.

THE DAILY NEWS

Lake Como

The Romans were here before we arrived
with our maps and our *Lonely Planet.*
Before them the Etruscans.
Before anyone, the slow grind of ice
gouging out sheer rock walls and a lake.

I like the long view back, the boulders
stranded in the wake of glaciers.
Those rocks are solid fact; they're not
going anywhere soon.

Yesterday rose and fell in a cloud of ash
and already the augurs are bringing reports
of tomorrow's war.
They're tracking the travel plans of birds.

And today: snow flurries in April!
No doubt an omen.
We rush out into the blur of snowflakes,
flustered and suddenly happy.
We're all set to hope
but the sky turns to water in our hands.

Wherever we land
there's sorrow and light, light and sorrow,
black and white Escher birds, beak-to-wing,
locked in flight.

THE GRAND CANYON

Flash after flash across the horizon:
tourists trying to take the canyon
by night. They don't know
every last shot will turn out black.

It takes sixty years for Rothko
to make his way to the rim.
He goes there only after dark.
As he stands at the railing, his pupils open
like a camera shutter at the slowest speed.

He has to be patient. He has to lean
far over the railing to see
the colors of darkness.
Purple, numb brown, mud-red, mauve
—a treasury of bruises.
At first he can see only black-on-black.
"Something you don't want to look at," he says.

As he waits,
the waves of color vibrate in the canyon
like voices.
                 Pilgrim, bring back something
from the brink
of nothing
                 to make us see.

II

THE DEAD OF NIGHT

An old memory comes home
in new clothing
at the dead of night,

turns a cold key in the lock.
A whiff
of camphor and Chanel.

Settles down in my best chair,
Don't let me disturb you,
and stakes its claim.

An old shame forgets what it came for.
An old fear scatters salt.
A young loss waits at the window.

An old grief whimpers and a new grief
kisses it. An intimate anger
takes off its clothes.

BEQUEST

If only you were my father, the child says
to his mother's lover.
A contrary-to-fact clause. The child
is hardly a child, he's twenty-five,
old enough to know the grammar
of second-guessing.

He's got to rake his way
through all the dead lives. With his sleeve
he wipes the sweat from his brow.

Imagine: once
our mothers and fathers were strangers
to each other! How strange they are,
looking down.
One hangs over the changing table
clucking and cooing,
one waves a little scepter that rattles.

They hover like a muggy sky.
Then the wind picks up
and their dust clings to us like a habit
there's no shaking off.

SWEEPING UP

The war is over now, and the field
lies in a litter of aftermath
—teacup and tablecloth,
Nitrostat, lipstick, the new Danielle Steele,
your misspelled DO NOT RESOSITATE,
the ordinary disorder.
I am your custodian, you have left me
to sweep up the leavings.

I've given the sofa away, but the dishes
are still in my basement, the rosebud dishes
I won't ever use. Your letters are fading
in the interrogative light of day
that bleaches everything it touches.

Tell me, mama: that amber ring
you bestowed with such solemnity,
—did you know it was glass?
What if we'd talked about the life after
tea and *mandelbroyt*,
where would that have taken us?
Did you ever find out if I was your child?

Your floral nightgown,
the one you hemmed in a hurry
with crooked stitches
—it fits. I'll admit: I keep wearing it.
I keep choosing to wear it.

What have you taken with you
that I might have used?

THE DISCIPLINE OF MARRIAGE

My mother said what she thought.
If my father looked up from the paper
to inquire, sotto voce,
where the hell anyone would get such a dumb idea,
she'd reply, with a smile like a warning:
"That's how I feel."

Her feelings were larger than his,
full of grievance, of steaming griefs.
She hung up her keys at the door
and salted the daily stew.

All day my father depleted his poor stock of words.
Evenings he shrank and fell silent.
The discipline of marriage had taught him
every last thing he knew about silence
and its rewards. After supper, he'd shut his eyes,
set his feet on the hassock and kiss
the evening goodbye.

My mother applied glittery blue to her eyelids.
Crystal bottles commanded her dressing table
with their flags of milky glass;
the French perfumes glowed like topaz.
She had plenty to say. She wanted him
to listen, to say something back! Open
his eyes for once and see her!
Her beaded purse! Her alligator shoes!

MIRROR, MIRROR

The body in the bedroom mirror
is my mother's,
the one I found so hopeless—
she could read my face—
when I was fifteen.

True, the breasts are better,
the nipples still rosy and alert,
but the stomach's the same tired pudding,
and those spider veins on the thighs.

Stand up straight. Tie your hair back.
Don't give me that look.
She was fifty, undressing; I was trying on
her satin, chiffon, gold lamé
America. That was the year she called me
a bookish girl from Russia
when I wouldn't wear lipstick.

Things are easier between us lately.
She's not so carping. Is even willing to listen.
One would almost think death
has mellowed her.

On my dresser, a photo of her at eighty,
tilting her head, leaning forward
—the better to see my life?
Her assessor's eye is shrewd but genial.
She has something crucial to tell me
but she's taking her own sweet time.

THE DARK OF DAY

We were trying to keep things neat and shiny.
Twenty-four years.
We had two sets of dishes—one for love,
one for hate. We kept them in separate cupboards.
Eat love and hate at the same meal
and you'll get punished.

The rabbis taught us the mathematics of dividing
this from that. They certified
the micro-moment when day tips over
into night: *When the third star presents itself in the sky.*
They drew a line through that eye of light, a longitude.
You've got to navigate the evening blessing
with precision, not one star too soon.
But night comes on slowly.
It takes all day.

My friend's father was killed
in a car crash. She hated him,
hadn't seen him in years.
When the police called, she drove to the ditch
where his wrecked Chevy waited for the tow-truck.

The body was gone. On the dashboard, broken glasses,
an open notebook splotched with his blood.
Then she was crying, not knowing why.
She tore out a stain on the mottled paper,
his ragged last breath,
and took it into her mouth.

WILD HONEY

A puddle of sun on the wooden floor.
The infant crawls to it, licks it,
dips a hand in and out,
letting the wild honey
trickle through his fingers.

Then that voice from on high—
Look at the pretty color!—
wipes up the glory with a rag of language.

THROUGH A GLASS

On the crown of his head
where the fontanelle pulsed
between spongy bones,
a bald spot is forming, globed and sleek
as a monk's tonsure.

I was the earliest pinch of civilization,
the one who laced him
into shoe leather
when he stumbled into walking upright.
"Shoes are unfair to children," he'd grouse.

Through a pane of glass
that shivers when the wind kicks up
I watch my son walk away.

He's out the door, up the street, around
a couple of corners by now.
I'm in for life.
He trips; my hand flies out;

I yank it back.

BLUE

The sky isn't really blue, it just looks blue
the way we looked happy in the family album.

So the grass isn't green either?
No, the grass is green
—or green enough in California
till summer burns it brown.
We call that gold.

And paper is white until it turns brittle.
What an odd compulsion, to preserve
the remains of the day
on paper. Paper!
When I turn the pages, bits of the old life
flake off in my hands,

a few worn hopes without punctuation
I once called love
as I lurched
from one hope to the next, irremediably
deep in blue.

Who could be happy in a life like that?
I was. It's true.
—The *real* truth, as we say, to distinguish it
from the other one.

LE SOIR QUI TOMBE

after Magritte

The burglar
pried the sash, shattered
the windowpane. Left shards of sun and sky
on the floor, invisible
prints on the sill.

Stripped the house bare and left
a sky framed in jagged glass.
Now it looks more naked than ever,
with one pock of sun
like an orange sticker: *You Are Here.*

After a man does that to me,
I wondered as a girl,
will the wind
blow into my body?

I sweep up the pieces of sun and sky.
New glass is cheap.
One pane, 2x3, a little putty,
some weatherproof paint, whatever will keep
the outside from seeping in.

And the house dreams up a healing
to fit the wound:
Whatever was torn, let it be mended
with this thin skin.

NATURAL HISTORY

It takes a long time to make a meadow.
First you need glaciers
to gouge out a lake.
Then reeds grow, the lake fills with silt
and eventually grass.

So many trees with their litter
of fallen leaves to beget
a single live joy.
Look at the dead ends
up and down that trunk: each one
could have been a branch.

So many miles between heart
and mouth.
               And the words fall
like belated raindrops
the day after a storm when you shake the tree,
if you happen to shake it.

III

TRESPASS

That man at the ticket counter has the look
of someone I loved
when I first started loving.
He's not the one, but he'll do.
I'm playing a god's game with him:
to see and not be seen.

Back then we played Adam and maiden,
marked every doorpost with virgin blood
For the first time ever.
Oh how we loved
to swear *We will always remember.*

Forgetting is the most cunning of locks
but it's only a lock. Tonight,
without knowing, that man
handed me a key.
I open him easily, helping myself
to whatever I please.

I'm here by myself this time, in memory's
second chance.
There's no stopping me now—nervy, elated,
I've sneaked past a sleepy guard
to plunder a time zone.

The man hasn't seen me. We won't even nod.
How could he know I have come
to take possession?

THE REMAINS

It's not his surprised body that appears, happily
unhesitating
under the apricot tree, but the tin
of peppermints
tucked in his back pocket.

Not his girlfriend's so-nicely-phrased advice
but the jiggly necklace of pencil stubs
she liked to wear.

Once again an inferior memory
has been installed, in place of
the one you could actually put to use.
You don't get to choose your dreams either.

And the past you lopped off with a pocketknife
that feverish afternoon
is still yours, conferred on you in perpetuity,
cramped and throbbing
like a phantom limb.

Sometimes you're tempted to kick
just to make sure it's no longer there.
Of course it's no longer there.
No reason why it should go on hurting.

TÊTE-À-TÊTE

We don't know each other. That's the best part.
That we won't meet again
is almost as good.

The sky is moonless—so close
we can reach up to adjust
the overhead stars

and take off from the world. It's quiet
except for the Boeing's dozy snore,
the weary drone of a thing

that has someplace to go
and follows its nose straight to the landing strip.
Let it rumble along in its sleep;

we can stay up all night!
We have no route map, no carry-ons,
no morning after,

only the lacy skies of Laissez-Passer
and our naked lives.
What a pleasure to meet

in the spacious intimacy
of strangers,
before shame is invented.

PRIVATE LIVES

I know a man who is always performing.
He has a limited repertoire.
If I ask, "Where are you going?"
he'll produce a smile
slick as a handshake.

His face is fully dressed and impeccably pleasing
but his wife's face is stripped
to bone and pain.
Whatever that man is trying to hide
the nakedness of her face uncovers.

Whenever the living room lights come on,
their private life is projected,
cropped by the window frame,
on a public screen.

Once my life, too, was Top Secret
common knowledge.
Strangers would season their day with my sorrows.
I was the salt of the evening meal.

Now it's my turn. I want to say,
Pull the shades! Don't let me see!
Instead I stand for as long as the moment lasts
in the comfortable dark,
letting the inside
look out.

SALVAGE

The master's asleep in his chair, his snore
a shrill trapped wind in the narrow hallway.
And on the bathroom sink, a pink-and-white
half-moon smile in a glass of water.
All night the smile persists
apart from him.

The nattering of clock, fridge, traffic, even
his creaky rocker—the world is getting louder.
At dinner he clicks his hearing aid
down into the ashtray.
Another door shut.

But the silence, isn't it oppressive?
I can't hear you, he answers, agreeably.
Each age has its privileges.

I'm ready to go, he's been saying.
We have all heard him say it.
But in the clammy torpor of four o'clock
he was mending a threadbare pillowcase
on the back porch today.
A few stitches will do it.

How can he leave? There are still
three soap-ends he glued into one
in the broken soap dish.
Under the hard hot rush of the faucet
it shrinks steadily in his hands.

A MANTLE

What she wants these days is to hurt
the world back. Bereavement
may keep her warm
and it's hers to wear as she bears him

into each day's cold.
Let a living man sing what he pleases,
a wife inherits
riddles and a stone. Grief

can be quarried and polished,
loss can be coined.
A widow is a bride of darkness,
like it or not.

She likes it. When he lived
she was smaller. Now she assumes
the great man's coat as though
she'd wrought it. Her anger at last
has found its calling.

WIDE OPEN

Take a deep breath, say the doctors, *don't blink,*
this won't hurt a bit.
What a honeysweet song they sing us.
But the eye refuses to believe. The eye
expects pain.

I wasn't blinking, not really. It was my body
that blinked. I
am wide open. I'm holding still.

Why are you talking so softly?
The better to see you.

Why are you talking so fast, what are you afraid of?
Me, afraid? I'll try anything once.
I'm old enough to know fear
is a salt the body craves.
Though suppose I get dizzy climbing
my fraying rope
in the slap of the wind—

You do like that feeling, don't you?
See that girl in the striped bathing suit?
We know who she is
on the slippery end of the diving board all summer,
counting to ten, counting,
taking a deep breath,
counting again.

THE NAKED FUTURE

We were sitting on my sofa with his dead wife.
(A good-looking woman, he allowed.)
All those women who wanted him.

On the sofa I saw a soldier of love
showing off his wounds and badges.
And what did he see?
I was tired of the future already, and we hadn't
started yet. We hadn't even started.

Sex is a brisk new broom. Tough, efficient.
It knows all the corners.

And that's how, one autumn evening, we began
dropping this-and-that onto the drafty floor
—history with its pockets, ticket-stubs, torn seams,
husbands and wives. He slipped off my watch
and laughed, "Oh, come on,"
when I stopped to pick up his blue shirt
and smooth it over the chair.

Then that implacable broom swept us bare.

PORTRAIT OF THE ARTIST

He showed me the painting he made of me
—at eighty? ninety? Clearly
he didn't mean to flatter.
Now he asks if I'm planning to write
a poem about him. He's smiling,
but under that brushed-on smile
he looks worried.

There's a couple of things he'd prefer to spare
the reading public.
Who wants to be published
stripped to his cotton socks,
with nothing but a fig leaf of metaphor
to keep him decent?

Sweetie, it's not you in the poem—it's you
ground to grist and pigment
with all the others. Don't you know
what a poet can do with a blank
sheet of paper? Words
are the poor man's colors.

Listen, I promise: I'll change your name.
And I'll never ask you to pose,
legs crossed at the ankle, eyes bright,
cheek nuzzling your hand.
Move all you want, I'll get you,
I've been getting you
all along.

A LONG WINTER'S NIGHT

The hands
are the hands of a young man making love
but his voice is parched.
I want to be
myself again, he tells me.

To be himself.
The way an old tree is green again
after the winter.
The way a tree that's cut down will bud
at the scent of water.

His hands are the hands of a lover.
When I see him drop them to cover himself
I understand winter and trees and bolts
on the inside of doors.

How can a woman understand? he asks
with blind hands
groping for green. I never saw
a man so naked.

WOMAN TALK

My friend is stone dry, though once
a love as wide as the Amazon
flooded and left her
pitted with gullies. That's how she tells it,
complaining, though it's half a boast.

You'd think she was telling a riddle:
What's big and dark and laps both its banks
and can spout such a rushing torrent
yet vanish so completely?

No use looking for desire now
on the barrens of her face.
You can almost touch
the cloud of dust that envelops her.

Men, she says, in a voice that reaches
for contempt but founders,
scraping itself
on the reef of his body.

There's got to be water somewhere.
If there's water, there may be life, I offer,
but it's hardly a comfort.
She watches me fumbling and laughs,
but it's hardly a laugh.

GREEN, GREEN

That thick mat of green lying
on the pond, how you'd love
to lie down and let it hold you,
float you away.
It grows like hair. Makes sugar
out of sun and air.

Your new man is like that. Green eyes
and a smile. He's beautiful, admit it.
You don't know his open face
is his cover. He's got his eyes
on you and his back to the wall.
He has no roots so he floats
at the edges, eats
wherever he can.

I need you, he says when he's hungry
so you give him a hand. He takes it.
Eats it. Then he's angry. You feed him
though you don't know how
you found him, how
those filaments twist together tight,
how they float to the surface.

You're studying algae, how it grows,
how it gulps the light.
It can kill a pond with a kiss.
I need you, he says in his green, green voice
and down you go.

TASHLICH

I start the new year by emptying my pockets
from the bridge in Live Oak Park.
Another year of crumbs.

Old sticky rancors I feed on in secret,
wadded tissues, *he saids* and *I saids*,
snarled hair, lint:
let the water take it!

What a muddle we make,
I with my swagger of *This time I mean it*,
all the while thinking *Maybe*
and other famous thoughts.
My right hand on the doorknob, resolute,
and the left
ready to warm itself in his pocket
till the end of days.

This time I mean it. As the bridge is my witness
and the water
under the bridge

and hard by the water, the snake
with its castoff story, its body stocking
sloughed in the dirt.

SIXTY O'CLOCK

Is it a ripsaw in plywood spitting
a burst of sawdust, a spray
of pent-up

woodchips? That nagging
two-note, is it a hopeless engine
that won't turn over,

or a bird? Could it be a bird?
Or a siren grinding
its monomaniacal

hardluck story at the corner
or closer, at the clouded
window I wake to?

The house is bone-cold when I get up.
I rattle inside it like ice cubes in the tray.
November. Any day now
will blow the trees bare.

And still, each morning, light stokes up
the red-leaf Japanese maple.

If it weren't so cold
I would go out and bow
to a fire like that. If the left hand
would not always push away
what the right pulls close. If the cold
were only
a little less cold—

A wild distance has caught
my scent, a distance that stops short
and listens.

LIVING WITH MYSELVES

They're up at all hours, the two of them,
sorting, pressing and folding
as they bundle the daily wash
in a plain gray wrapper.
They're always losing something.
What they deliver is full of holes,
I'm not sure it's even mine.

The left doesn't know what the right is doing.
One has a heart; one does the chores.
When things get tough, I hear them go at it:
"I can't live with that." "I can."

But on the nights when they're screening
the dream of the secret room,
I'm ready to forgive everything.
"A room in hiding! Right in our house!"
"How did you miss it till now?"

Each time the dream is different.
Louvered windows and a bare wooden floor
or a plush carpet with the luster of opal
—is that room dreaming me?
A doorknob slides into my hand
and the house starts to grow.

"This is the life you haven't lived,"
says the prickly one.
"This is your life," says the other. "It's time
you had a look around."

THE COLOR GREEN

Two floors up, at the corner of Hearst and Oxford,
he's clamped for good
in an iron lung. When it's time to eat
he nudges his head a sweaty mile
to the edge of the pillow. It takes a while.

His brilliant bloodshot light-blue eyes
steer me from cupboard to fridge:
he would like his chicken burrito
cut into bite-size pieces,
a bent straw for his glass of water, please.

How does the body live its only life
in a cage? I watch him compute the distance
from bar to bar, and squeeze
between them
with a violent compression, a fury of bursting free
that doesn't last.

His will is a crowbar, angled to pry up
the rooted intractable weight
of matter. I watch him slyly, I check out
the way he does it. He
does it. But pain in its absolute privacy
weighs what it weighs.

I come here to study the soul, posing one question
a dozen ways, most of them silent.
"If I'm only a body," he laughs,
"I'm up shit creek." His laugh
a gritty eruption of rock, salt and breath.

Like me he writes poems
but he does it letter by letter
on a propped keyboard, the mouth-stick
wobbling between his teeth.
That kind of speed keeps a poet accountable.
He won't ever say "The grass is very green"
when it's only green.

THE SIXTH AGE

Words slip from me lately
like cups and saucers
from soapy hands.
I grope for the names of things
that are governed, like me, by the laws
of slippage and breakage.

I am like a child
left behind by the fast-talking
grownups. A tourist
lost in the blind alleys
of a foreign language.

How will I see my way to anywhere
without my words?

I slam up and down the stairs of our house:
Where are my glasses hiding?
Rimless, invisible as oxygen.
I need glasses to find them.

There must be words left
to go on searching for the ones I've lost

the way the blind man I once loved
found me,
first with his fingertips,
then with his whole hand.

OU SONT LES NEIGES

Grizzled old clumps by the roadside
salted and sanded
nasty with ice

Who'd ever know
how fresh-in-the-world we lay
new-fallen, moist
If any man ventured by
he'd give himself away

With each gust we grow
more pocked with grime
belly buttock and breast
And the poet says
Have ye made much of Time
What of your dancing days

Who would guess
we were yesterday's darlings
Ah, my dear
we shrink into yesteryear

The air is filling with soft and softer flakes
sweet look-alikes
each one unique
And the geese fly over, crying
New snow
New snow

A BURIED LANGUAGE

"If you catch it early—." The nurse
made a cheerful motion,
plucking a thorn from the air,
then pressed a solemn hand to her breast
like pledging allegiance.

She was teaching my hand to read
a buried language, to grope for
a knot of consonants tough as gristle,
hard as a full stop.
"Armpit to bra line, sternum
to collarbone."

Each month again
steam fills the shower; my hand
slips into its glove of soap.

You must do this, my mind
lectures the hand that feeds me,
that does my bidding, that is able
to write these poems,

but each month again my hand,
my capable good right hand
that could save me
backs away.

THE BULLET

passed through her brain at an acute angle
and lodged in the soft tissue
of our lives.

It was then we knew her,
mantle and magma.

Last Tuesday, in her plaid suit, she looked
—what did we call it, happy?
though strictly speaking, she was invisible.

Now, in the searchlight of her death, I can make out
her hand, her fingers, the barrel clamped
between her teeth. I can taste it,
that bulking metal. It makes me gag.

I go on arguing with her back.
How easy it is, she answers
without turning. *A crook of the finger,
a puff of smoke.*
                              Grief
is a strange anger. I want to grab her,
twist her trigger arm
hard.

ENVY

"Damned if I don't fight," Naomi swore
and I envied the way she said it.

She wanted to run downstairs,
pare an apple, dip her spoon in the sauce.
Wipe her own ass
and tie her shoelaces.
She was planning the battle from her hospital bed.
And I, of sound body and greedy heart—
I envied the way she said it.

Then she died and became
available to us.
I sit with the others and take
her life in my hands. The silky
feel of her secrets. She wanted to have
a child. To have children. She even—

A week ago she was reaching
for the ancient bottle of Jean Naté,
citron yellow
beside a glassful of purple asters,
a little still life on the bedside table.
"Would you rub my shoulders with cologne."

I swabbed her with long sweet lemon strokes,
a ritual washing of the body
this side of death.
When I finished, she looked almost happy.
She had only a few wishes left by then,
each one smaller than the last.

A SHOW OF RED

Eduardo tied a red ribbon around my wrist.
Close your eyes.
Make a wish.
Don't tell.
And he tied a triple knot.

Every table in that café broadcast
its own commotion
of spoons, forks, lives.
Inside me a dry metallic scraping.

I made a wish in the privacy
of my closed eyelids—believing, of course,
as the ribbon required.
From that moment the wish took breath
like a cricket throbbing in my fist.

I moved among people and kept
repeating the wish to myself.
What's that ribbon for? they asked,
but I was so dutiful (so desperate, I mean),
I was the only one I told.

The ribbon was simply a show of red
that shriveled to a knotted string.
Two and a half years
that ribbon kept waking me.
And the wish grew more hungry
as I fed it, in secret,
one silence at a time.

BLOOD HONEY

Apprehended and held without trial,
our friend was sentenced:
brain tumor, malignant.
Condemned each day to wake
and remember.

Overnight, a wall sprang up around him,
leaving the rest of us
outside.

Death passed over us this time.
We're still at large. We're free
to get out of bed, start the coffee,
open the blinds.
The first of the human freedoms.

If he's guilty
we must be guilty; we're all made of
the same cup of dust—

It's a blessing, isn't it? To be able,
days at a time,
to forget what we are.

*

These numbered days
have a concentrated sweetness
that's pressed from us,
the dying man most of all.

Today we eat brunch at Chester's,
poached egg on toast,
orange juice foaming in frosted glasses.

He remembers the summer he packed blood oranges,
stripped to the waist,
drinking the fresh-squeezed juice in the factory
straight from the tap.
He cups his left hand under his chin
as if to a faucet, laughing.

He is scooping sweetness from the belly of death
—honey from the lion's carcass.

We sit with our friend
and brood on the riddle he sets before us:
What is it, this blood honey?

       *

A shadow is eating the sun.
It can blind you
but he's looking right at it,
he won't turn away.

Already his gaze is marked
by such hard looking,
though just now he asked,
plaintive as a child,
Why won't it go away?

Day after day breaks
and gives him
back to us
broken.

Soon the husk of his knowing
won't know even that.

*

A man lies alone in his body in a world
he can still desire.
Another slice of pie? he asks.

As long as he's hungry
he's still one of us.
Oh Lord, not yet.

He drums out a jazz beat on the bedrail
with his one good hand
when the words stumble.
See? he says. *I can trick the tumor.*

He can still taste and see.
The world is good.

He hauls himself up in bed,
squinting his one good eye at the kingdom
through a keyhole
that keeps getting smaller
and smaller.
It is good. It is very good.

V

THE KNOWN FACTS

You wake to the sloped ceiling,
to bedclothes steeped in moonlight.
If you start looking out the window now,
forget about sleep.

The known facts about him
are stones in a stream; it's the way you proceed
from here to there.
In the moonlight of your imaginings
the stones are slippery.

Other women have lifted their skirts
to stumble across, and you don't know
their story, either.

The unknown facts have dominion
over night and day.
Have you already managed to forget,
girl? That force of gravity
governed the sky of your marriage,
its exploding stars—

a mass of dark matter
no one could see.

ON THE SHORTEST DAY OF THE YEAR

I love the bare trees that let me see them.
In winter I know what they are,
the articulation of the branches
down to the smallest twig.

Let the frozen pond
keep its secrets to itself.
The trees are open, full of sky, the forest
finally visible—

I can see past the pillars of sepia and snow,
past the fallen deadwood,
deep into the thicket.

That's how I want to know you,
in that clear a light.

THE CUNNING OF HUNGER

A fox is worrying the wild turkeys in the meadow.
At last count one hen, nine chicks and a fox.
I've watched the chicks line up sweetly
to cross the meadow,
the fox a red-tailed streak in the grass.
The cunning of hunger makes him almost invisible.

You are way out of reach. Which leaves me
to brood about lust,
how it streaks from seeing to eating,
and the slow monotonous grind that sharpens
lust from a distance. How the body
has a mind of its own, and hunger
outfoxes our nimble wits.

Wherever you happen to be tonight,
be warned:
across a few thousand fields of standing grass
I am setting out now, *now*
to devour you.

CURB

Five miles out of London, we slam
into the curb, swerve away. Rotten
misshapen foreign curb. Our nerves
register the angle of impact; the car is careening; shouldn't we—

Stop! The front tire is sinking steadily.
A chilly wind frisks us.
Then the rain begins, impersonal.
We feel singled out.

By now we're trading syllables of surgical steel.
Hand me the jack. Where's the jack?

Limping off on the narrow spare, we are meager
with one another, immoderately polite.
We take turns saying nothing,
the static more viscous with each agitation.
It sticks to everything.

Rain nags the windshield. Won't let up.
All day the unspoken drizzles its own sullen weather.

SOMETIMES I WANT TO SINK INTO YOUR BODY

Sometimes I want to sink into your body
with the fever that spikes inside me
to be a woman
who can open a man.

Why must I be only softness and haunches,
a satin cul-de-sac?

You ought to know what sharpens me
like a barbed arrow.
Do you think we're so different?

How you tease me, twiddle me,
hustle me along,
just when I'd like to splay you
tooth and nail.

AFTER SEX

A man after sex
has that squishy thing in the nest of his lap.
A bashful appendage
like a Claes Oldenburg vinyl drainpipe,
a soft saxophone that won't toot a note.

A man's got to wear his susceptibility
out in plain sight.
No wonder he's keeping his soul
zippered up.

A woman's got that rock of a belly,
that baby cave,
breasts swaggering erect
when they swell with milk.
Oh she knows what it's like to sing
the stand-up song of a man.

Now you and I soften in the wash,
the body-elastic goes slack.
We see ourselves in each other,
we grow alike.
We want to curl up in a sunny corner
and doze like the cat.

Come, flick a whisker,
make me remember.

SONNET ENDING WITH A LINE BY DAVE

A landscape spiked with thistles
the gray-brown of weathered wood
—our sign for persistence,
like the bristly stubble underfoot.

That's how it was when we met at sixty:
we and our skeptical resolute
autumn kisses,
testing out *can't* and *could.*

When you were young
you were given an answer
it's taken the whole of our lives to decipher.

Hunger is a shrewd teacher,
we learn, being poor.
Love is the youth we hunger for.

ROOTS

Even as we speak, our silences
are beginning to root themselves.
Blind little feelers,
they move with a sly persistence
till an unspoken word strikes water.
Or stone.

As for that leafy business in the sky,
that dazzle and jostle—
it's harmless,
a benign friction that passes for speech
though public, and not their own:
the leaves repeat
only what the wind has told them.

Even as we speak, the roots
are pressing their questions, reaching
deeper into silence.
Each day they grow denser and more detailed
in their grasp of the dark.

ANTEROOM

"I don't want to alarm you, but . . . . "
   Don't
     but
strikes the eardrum first. And then
   that ellipsis
trailing its wake of silence.
What? what?

Tonight you have been detained
in the holding tank of gel and electrodes
where a stylus monitors your quaking.
Again you are made
to repeat your name.

In the hush and babble of the ER
the whitecoats
hover and confer.

Lucky you! Not a single positive
this time.
    You may go home
to that other life with its comforting clatter,
you've rehearsed
the required emotions.

Once again you have passed the test
for the wrong disaster.

THE WEIGHT

The mind is counting its losses again,
the hand groping for a comfort
heavy enough to serve.

On the empty pan of the balance
we lay a stone,
Could have been worse,

weighing the dark of the day
against a larger
life-sinking dark.

THE SIXTH TRUMPET

after Anselm Kiefer

Lately we've begun to talk logistics,
to draw up contingency plans
for a war we're preparing
to lose. We're counting backwards

from D-day. *If I die first*, we tell each other.
Sometimes: *If you die first*. Declarations
flare in the street, the museum.
Our children can't stand that kind of talk,

they announce in front of Kiefer's painting.
They see an immense plowed field
under a day sky seeded with dark stars.
Sunflower seeds! they say. *He used real seeds.*

We see a bombardment of cinders
that fall through the air onto furrows
of emulsion, acrylic, shellac
to converge on a vanishing point.

No place to hide from the sky
—we'd better prepare a shelter
for them. We dole out small truths,
sufficient unto the day.

Sunflower seeds, we say.

VENI VIDI

The world
is about to be created.

Today the streets are empty. The shops
are getting a fresh coat of paint
behind metal shutters.

Even the weather isn't ready:
unseasonable frost,
though the greens of spring are just beginning
to probe the hardpan of winter.

In the piazza there's a single palm tree,
gawky as Big Bird,
its fronds wrapped in a canvas bustle,
one green tuft poking up like a tail.
It's being groomed for the season.
They'll let it out soon
when more of our kind arrive.

We're leaving on the ferry
after the new ones disembark.

We still have time
to dash off a swaggering
Veni vidi on glossy postcards:
We came, we saw
the Tourist Bureau sign
THIS WAY TO THE SUNSET,
the lake with its fresh coat of light.

A LIFE ON EARTH

Bury me in that cemetery on Fairmount
across from Fat Apple's
where deer come to eat the flowers of the newly dead,
reds and purples, fresh from the florist.
A buck takes a whole bouquet in his mouth,
then gazes steadily at me.

It's a royal park—live oak, eucalyptus, pine—
with a view of two bridges and the Bay.
I like to walk in the presence of the dead.
It clears my mind.

*

An adult heart is the size of a fist, he said.

And what does the heart do?
Hoists itself up each morning into the weather.
A fist is not just a sign of defiance:
four fingers and a thumb can grasp. And hold.

And what does the heart hold in that tight little fist?
The string of its one life on earth,
taking the tug of it, letting it fly,
not letting it fly away.

*

A dribble of dirt, of clods on wood.
The shovel passed hand-to-hand,

the coffin lid
a shiny door we were pelting shut.

We stood subdued and stared
at the ground.

I took home that odd
percussive thud.

*

Last time we talked about the afterlife,
we ended up snapping: "Arrogance!"
"Ignorance!" "Wishful thinking!"

Someday, I'll be a little pile of dust,
said Elihu to Job
with his sour smile. *And you'll be
a beam of light.*

NOTES AND APPRECIATIONS

BROTHERS
lifted my hand: "And Abraham stretched forth his hand, and took the knife to slay his son." (Gen. 22:10).

THE MESSIAH OF HARVARD SQUARE
For Rabbi Ben-Zion Gold.

FLOUR AND ASH
For Berkeley artist Gale Antokal.

COVENANT
live coal: "Then flew one of the seraphim unto me, having a live coal in his hand, which he had taken with the tongs from off the altar. And he laid it upon my mouth, and said, Lo, this hath touched thy lips" (Isaiah 6:6-8).

THE GRAND CANYON
The Rothko Chapel, in Houston, Texas, displays fourteen large dark paintings by Mark Rothko (1903-70), the work of his last six years.

TASHLICH
"Thou wilt cast away" (Hebrew). A symbolic act of repentance on Rosh Hashanah, the Jewish New Year, when Jews traditionally cast breadcrumbs into a stream, reciting Micah 7:19, "Thou wilt cast all their sins into the depths of the sea."

THE COLOR GREEN
In memory of Berkeley poet and journalist Mark O'Brien (1949-99), a guiding spirit in the movement of disabled people to lead independent lives. Mark was the subject of an award-winning documentary film by Jessica Yu, *Breathing Lessons: The Life and Work of Mark O'Brien.*

ENVY
In memory of Naomi Kies (1942-85), American-Israeli peace activist.

BLOOD HONEY
In loving memory of Amichai Kronfeld (1947-2005), philosopher, jazz musician, peace activist.
honey from the lion's carcass, riddle: "Out of the eater came forth meat, and out of the strong came forth sweetness. . . . What is sweeter than honey? And what is stronger than a lion?" (Judges 14:5-18).

THE SIXTH TRUMPET
Anselm Kiefer's *Die sechste Posaune* (1996). The title alludes to Revelation 9:13-21, an apocalyptic vision of mass destruction.

I am grateful to the Bellagio Study Center, the Djerassi Foundation, the MacDowell Colony, and the Corporation of Yaddo for rewarding residencies during which the poems in *Blood Honey* were written or revised.

Many dear friends have offered valuable criticism of these poems. For their demanding critique of the final manuscript, I particularly wish to thank Andrea Hollander Budy, Tess Gallagher, and Barry and Lorrie Goldensohn. My deepest gratitude to Anita Barrows, Chana Kronfeld, and Dave Sutter, always my first-and-last readers.

Finally, it is a pleasure to thank Michael Simms of Autumn House Press for his discerning attention to matters large and small, and his superb editing.

THE AUTUMN HOUSE POETRY SERIES

The Leaving, New and Selected Poems by Sue Ellen Thompson
Dirt by Jo McDougall
Fire in the Orchard by Gary Margolis
▲ *Just Once, New and Previous Poems* by Samuel Hazo
The White Calf Kicks by Deborah Slicer • 2003, selected by
  Naomi Shihab Nye
The Divine Salt by Peter Blair
▲ *The Dark Takes Aim* by Julie Suk
Satisfied with Havoc by Jo McDougall
Half Lives by Richard Jackson
▲ *Not God After All* by Gerald Stern (with drawings by Sheba Sharrow)
Dear Good Naked Morning by Ruth L. Schwartz • 2004, selected by
  Alicia Ostriker
▲ *A Flight to Elsewhere* by Samuel Hazo
Collected Poems by Patricia Dobler
The Autumn House Anthology of Contemporary American Poetry,
  edited by Sue Ellen Thompson
Déjà Vu Diner by Leonard Gontarek
Lucky Wreck by Ada Limón • 2005, selected by Jean Valentine
The Golden Hour by Sue Ellen Thompson
Woman in the Painting by Andrea Hollander Budy
Joyful Noise: An Anthology of American Spiritual Poetry edited by
  Robert Strong
No Sweeter Fat by Nancy Pagh • 2006, selected by Tim Seibles
Unreconstructed: Poems Selected and New by Ed Ochester
Rabbis of the Air by Philip Terman
The River Is Rising by Patricia Jabbeh Wesley
Let It Be a Dark Roux by Sheryl St. Germain
Dixmont by Rick Campbell
The Dark Opens by Miriam Levine • 2007, selected by Mark Doty
▲ *The Song of the Horse* by Samuel Hazo
My Life as a Doll by Elizabeth Kirschner
She Heads into the Wilderness by Anne Marie Macari
*When She Named Fire: An Anthology of Contemporary Poetry by American
  Women* edited by Andrea Hollander Budy
67 Mogul Miniatures by Raza Ali Hasan
House Where a Woman by Lori Wilson
A Theory of Everything by Mary Crockett Hill • 2008, selected by
  Naomi Shihab Nye
What the Heart Can Bear by Robert Gibb
Blood Honey by Chana Bloch

  • Winner of the annual Autumn House Poetry Prize
  ▲ Hardcover

DESIGN AND PRODUCTION

Text and cover designed by Kathy Boykowycz
Cover art: Kate Cheney Chappell, "Vessels; La Semaine,"
  mixed media installation, 2006

Set in Lucida fonts, designed in 1987 by Kris Holmes

Printed by Thomson-Shore of Dexter, Michigan
  on Nature's Natural, a 40% recycled paper